EAST WEST HEALTH BOOKS
17 Station Street
Brookline, MA 02146

ISBN 0-936184-05-1

Library of Congress No. 86-081294

Printed in the United States of America

First Edition

4 6 8 9 7 5

*Distributed to the natural food trade by
East West Books, 17 Station Street, Brookline, MA 02146
and to the book trade by
The Talman Co., 150 Fifth Avenue, New York, NY 10011*

*Design by Paola Di Stefano
Illustrations by James Steinberg*

*Design Electronically Implemented and Typeset
Using Software from AT&T and
Textware International*

Sweet & Natural
D·E·S·S·E·R·T·S

East West's Best and Most Wholesome, Sugar- and Dairy-Free Treats

from the Editors of East West Journal

EAST WEST HEALTH BOOKS

CONTENTS

3

PASTRIES

4

PIES

5

COOKIES

6

CAKES

7

CREPES

8

SWEET BREADS

9

SAUCES, FILLINGS, & FROSTINGS

10

CANDIES & SNACKS

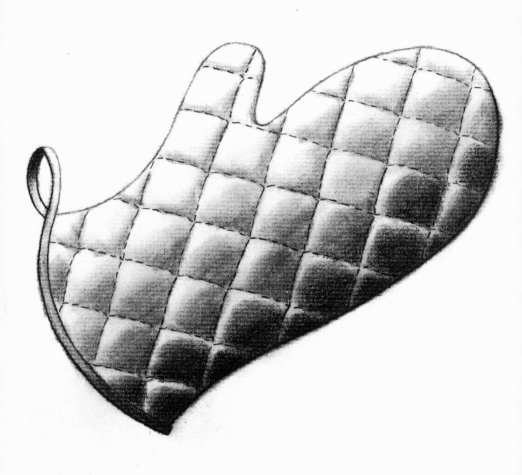

INTRODUCTION

any of us have a love-hate
relationship with desserts. We look forward to indulging in the luxurious
sweetness of pies, cakes, cobblers, puddings, and cookies, but all too often we
feel guilty afterward—or sick.

It need not be so. In this collection from the cooking columns of *East West
Journal* we offer desserts using only whole, natural ingredients. As the finale to
special meals, or by themselves as extra-ordinary treats, these delicious
confections can be served with pride and eaten with confidence.

In addition to creating the recipes, the experienced cooks who contributed to this
compilation offered their suggestions for success. Without exception , their first
admonishment was to be creative—don't get locked into trying to exactly
reproduce someone else's recipe. If your pantry doesn't contain a specific
ingredient (among the obvious variables such as fruits and sweeteners), or if you
have a preference for something else, don't be afraid to substitute or embellish.

Learn to understand the individual characteristics of basic ingredients, as well as
how they act in combination with others. For instance, for the sake of final
consistency maple syrup might be your choice as a sweetener rather than barley
malt syrup or rice malt syrup. When using dried fruits—raisins, currants, apricots,
and so forth—it is best to rinse them and then soak them overnight or for several
hours in water to cover. They can then be cooked for a few minutes to allow
them to soften and release their flavor before they are combined with other
ingredients. The soaking or cooking liquid should be used in recipes that call for
"a little water."

When grating citrus rind, never grate it down to the white. Use a light touch and rotate the fruit after each stroke. You want just the essence of flavor—not the strong bitterness the white will impart. Using the rind is a good reason to buy organic fruit.

Since certain ingredients such as yeast and baking powder will vary in quality, and each oven has its own idiosyncrasies, expect that a new recipe may need a testing or two before it turns out the way you like it.

A professional dessert-maker we know says that he gets the best results when he uses the lowest possible oven temperature and the shortest possible baking time. It is a very fine line, he says, but over-baking is to be avoided at all costs. Even a minute or two, or a few degrees, might make the difference between a dessert that is mediocre and one that is superb. For this reason, as well as for ease of digestion and balance of flavors, try for a very thin pie crust. Many a lovely filling has been overpowered by a thick, over- or under-cooked crust. In general, make the top crust even thinner than the bottom.

Think about the weather—is it cold and rainy, or hot and dry? On a rainy day make your desserts and breads a little drier, and on dry days make them a little moister. It is a subtle difference, but diners are always appreciative—even when they're not sure why. And of course on a hot day in summer a light fruit dessert tastes and feels better than a baked pastry.

Most baked and well-cooked fruit desserts taste better the day after they are made. The flavors blend and the overall effect is richer. Desserts using kanten, however, should be served very fresh to take advantage of their lightness.

Most of the "exotic" ingredients used in these recipes—such as agar or kanten, kuzu, rice syrup, and so forth—are readily available at natural and whole foods stores across the country and worldwide. They are all nutritious foods as well as delicious dessert ingredients.

Bon appetit! Special thanks to *East West Journal* staff members Leonard Jacobs, Mary Colson, Linda Roszak, Mark Mayell, and Meg Seaker, to Joanne Saltzman and Barbara Jacobs for their organizational help, and especially to *East West*'s cooking column contributors: Karen Acuff, Kathleen Bellicchi, Robert N. Carr, Jr., Annemarie Colbin, Barbara Coons, Mary Estella, Neil Garland, Barbara Jacobs,

Janet Lacey, Derbhail Leonard, Lynda LeMole, Barbara Liddle, Joan Livingston, Isobel O'Donnell, Lynne Paterson, Pieter, Ann Rawley, Carol Schoenberger, William Shurtleff, Hilary Stillman, Jean Strong, Gerry Thompson, Marcea Newman Weber, Rebecca Wood, and Ruth Zablotsky.

1

SIMPLY FRUIT

APPLE DELIGHT

his healthful dessert is a natural throughout the fall and winter. Its preparation is so simple that even the busiest schedule can accommodate it. Serves 3-4.

4 McIntosh or Cortland apples

⅓ cup water

pinch sea salt

1 tablespoon lemon juice

½ teaspoon grated lemon rind

Quarter the apples, remove the cores, and cut each quarter in half lengthwise. Place the slices in a saucepan, and add water and salt. Bring to a simmer over a low flame. Remove the apples from the heat and add the lemon juice and rind. Stir gently, taking care that the apples are not broken. Cool the apples to room temperature and refrigerate them until serving time.

DRIED FRUIT COMPOTE

Serve old-fashioned compote any time of day. It is satisfying in itself and also makes a superb topping for cakes and puddings. Serves 5.

*1 cup each dried prunes, apricots, and apples or
3 cups mixed dried fruit of your choice*

½ cup raisins

8 cups water

2 cinnamon sticks

½ cup almonds or sunflower seeds

grated coconut or roasted almonds, to garnish (optional)

Combine all ingredients in saucepan and bring to a boil. Cover the pot and simmer for 45 minutes. Serve the fruit hot, at room temperature, or chilled. Top with grated coconut, Tofu "Whipped Cream" (page 105), Tofu Mocha Creme (page 104), or roasted almonds.

APPLES WITH
APRICOT SAUCE

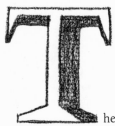he distinct flavors of apricots, apples, and walnuts enhance each other in this original, saucy dessert.

*1½ cups dried apricots — soaked in water
to cover, for 1 hour or more*

*6 small apples — washed, halved,
cored, and peeled if desired*

pinch sea salt

½ pound toasted walnuts, chopped

Place the soaked apricots and their soaking water in a saucepan with a pinch of sea salt. Cover, and cook at a low boil for 15 to 20 minutes or until tender, adding more water as needed to prevent sticking. Place the apples in a covered saucepan with ½ inch water and simmer for 5-10 minutes until they are tender but still keeping their shape. Cut or mash the apricots, and add juice from the apples to make a thick sauce, adding additional water as needed.

To serve, spoon a small amount of the apricot sauce over the apples, and top with the chopped walnuts.

Core the apples and leave whole. Cut an X into the skin on the tops of the apples to prevent the skin from bursting. Bake them for about 20 minutes at 350° F.

Use peeled peaches or pears. Briefly simmer the fruit in a combination of half water and half rice malt syrup, barley malt syrup, or maple syrup. Flavor with a little grated lemon rind.

Top with toasted seeds, nuts, or crunchy granola (page 112).

Make sauces with raisins, currants, prunes, or other dried or fresh fruits, adding citrus juice or rind, thickeners (agar, arrowroot, or kuzu), or spices.

Leftover fruit sauce makes a great jam.

STEWED PEACHES

*T*he perfect dessert for young cooks to present to their families. Stewed peaches can be enlivened with a sprinkling of granola (page 112). Serves 6-8.

10 fresh ripe peaches

water

2 teaspoons vanilla extract

lightly grated rind of 1 lemon

Wash the peaches and cut them in half lengthwise. Remove the pits and cut each half into three slices. In a saucepan, cover the slices of peaches with water and add the vanilla extract and lemon rind. Bring the water to a boil, then lower the heat and simmer, covered, for 5 minutes. Serve at room temperature or chilled.

GLAZED PEARS

simple but elegant finish to any meal, this warm dessert is especially welcome on a chilly winter night. Serves 4.

4 ripe pears ❖ *8 whole cloves*

1 cup apple juice ❖ *pinch sea salt*

1 tablespoon kuzu

½ teaspoon grated ginger

Preheat the oven to 350° F. Cut the pears in half and place them in a baking dish, cut side up. Press a clove into the center of each half. Pour apple juice over the pears, and cover the pan. Bake the pears for 15 minutes, then check them for tenderness. If necessary, return them to the oven and continue to bake, checking them at 5 minute intervals until they are tender.

Drain the juice from the pears into a small saucepan. Mix a small amount of this liquid with the kuzu and stir until all the kuzu is dissolved. Add the rest of the liquid, the salt, and the grated ginger. Cook the mixture over medium heat, stirring until it thickens and becomes clear. Pour this glaze over the pears and return them to the oven for 15 minutes.

FRUIT SALAD

ight and colorful, fruit salad is appreciated every season of the year. This version is especially suitable for the summer months. Serves 8.

6 ripe peaches ❖ *8 ripe apricots*

1 bunch grapes (seedless green)

1 large or 2 small cantaloupes ❖ *rosehip tea*

chopped fresh mint or spearmint,
for garnish

Cut the peaches into bite-size pieces and the apricots into small wedges. Cut the grapes in half and remove the seeds if seedless grapes are not available. Cut the melon in half, remove the seeds, and slice it into wedges. Slice off the rind and cut the melon into bite-size pieces, or use a melon-ball cutter. Combine the fruit in a large bowl.

Brew 2 cups of tea. When it is cool, add the chopped mint or spearmint. Pour the tea over the fruit. Refrigerate for at least an hour before serving in individual small bowls garnished with sprigs of fresh mint.

Conventional "fruit cocktail" is usually made with a sugary syrup. In this recipe, the tea provides a delightful freshness and a medium for blending the flavors of the fruit.

HALLOWEEN SURPRISE

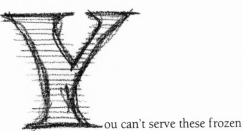

ou can't serve these frozen surprises to trick or treaters, but you can use them to brighten up a spooky party. Serves 6.

10 oranges

2 tablespoons tahini

½ teaspoon vanilla extract

Extract 2 cups juice from the oranges. Thoroughly blend ½ cup orange juice and the tahini in a blender. Transfer to a 1-quart bowl and stir in the remaining juice and the vanilla. Pour the mixture into small paper cups and freeze overnight.

To make frozen treats, place sticks or wooden ice cream spoons in the cups when the mixture has started to thicken.

Satisfy hot weather longings for a refreshing cooler with this frozen melon and citrus treat, spiced with a hint of mint. Yields 12 servings.

3 cups watermelon purée

1 cup cantaloupe purée ❖ *½ teaspoon sea salt*

1 teaspoon lime, lemon, or orange juice

1 cup water ❖ *1 teaspoon mint leaves*

Remove seeds from the melons and purée the fruits in a food mill or blender until you have 3 cups watermelon and 1 cup cantaloupe purée. Place the purées in a saucepan and add the salt and citrus juice. Simmer 15 minutes.

In a separate saucepan, cook the water and mint leaves together, uncovered, for 3 minutes. Strain out the leaves and add this mint tea concentrate to the melon mixture.

Line muffin tins with paper cupcake liners. Pour the melon mixture into them, and place in the freezer. When the fruit is partially frozen, insert sticks and return to the freezer until the treats are hard.

APRICOT SHERBET

he tantalizing tartness of ripe apricots combines with the creaminess of blended tofu to yield a smooth and refreshing dessert. Serves 6.

1 bar kanten or
2 tablespoons agar flakes

1 ¾ cups apple juice

1 cup apricots, pitted fresh or stewed

one 16 oz. cake tofu, crumbled

Rinse the kanten bar under cool water and squeeze it dry. Pour the juice into a saucepan and shred the kanten into the juice. If agar flakes are used, sprinkle them over the surface of the juice. They do not require soaking or rinsing.

Bring the juice to a boil over a medium heat. Reduce the heat and simmer for 3 to 4 minutes, or until the kanten is dissolved, stirring occasionally. Pour the juice into a blender, add the apricots and tofu, and process until smooth. Freeze until firm but not solid.

2

PUDDINGS

ORANGE CUSTARD

reamy and cool with hints of cinnamon and ginger, this custard can double as a topping for Stephen's Layered Carrot Cake (page 72) or Easy Lemon-Walnut Bread (page 93). Serves 8-10.

4 cups apple juice ❖ *1 cup rice syrup*

½ cup tahini (optional) ❖ *1 teaspoon grated orange rind*

1 teaspoon juice from peeled, grated fresh ginger

¼ teaspoon cinnamon ❖ *½ teaspoon salt*

3 bars kanten ❖ *2 cups orange juice*

2 tablespoons arrowroot powder or kuzu

almonds or walnuts, for garnish

In a large saucepan, combine the first seven ingredients. Shred or break up the kanten bars, stir them into the mixture, and let soak for 30 minutes. Place the pot over medium heat, bring to a boil, and let cook for 3 minutes. Add orange juice with arrowroot or kuzu dissolved in it, bring to a boil again, and let cook for only 30 seconds.

Let the mixture cool. Just before it sets, whip it in a blender or use a whisk to briskly whip it by hand. Pour into serving glasses and let cool before serving. Decorate with a lightly roasted single or chopped almond or walnut.

APPLE MOUSSE

op this thickened applesauce with a dollop of Tofu "Whipped Cream" (page 105) for a luxurious fall pudding. Serves 4.

8 medium McIntosh apples

1 cup water ❖ *1 tablespoon vanilla extract*

lightly grated rind of ½ lemon ❖ *pinch sea salt (optional)*

5 tablespoons kuzu or 10 tablespoons arrowroot powder,
dissolved in ½ cup water

chopped, roasted almonds, for garnish

Peel, quarter, and core the apples. Place the pieces in a covered 3-quart pot with ½ cup water. Cook over a low heat for 20 minutes or until the apples become soft. Stir occasionally to break up the pieces.

Add the vanilla and lemon rind to the apples; add salt if the apples are tart. Dissolve the kuzu or arrowroot in ½ cup water and add to the hot apples, stirring the mixture constantly until it comes to a boil and thickens. Continue to stir for 2 minutes. Remove the apples from the heat and allow them to cool. Serve individual portions garnished with the chopped, roasted almonds.

AMAZAKE

his traditional Japanese preparation derives its irresistible sweetness only from grain — usually sweet rice, a glutinous variety of rice — that has been fermented by koji. Koji, a grain or bean inoculated with Aspergillus oryzae mold, breaks down the complex carbohydrates of the grains, resulting in amazake's ease of digestibility and delicious taste. Serves 6.

The following basic recipe yields a pudding that may be flavored with vanilla, fruits, spices, nuts, carob powder, and so forth. Amazake also makes an excellent "custard" filling for Dream Puffs (page 42).

1½ cups sweet rice

3½ cups water ❖ *½ cup koji rice*

pinch sea salt

Combine the sweet rice and water in a pressure cooker and bring to full pressure. Reduce the heat and cook for 1 hour. (If boiling, use 4½ cups water, cover tightly, and cook for 1½ hours over a low heat.) Remove from the heat and set the pot aside to allow the pressure to return to normal.

Turn the rice out into a large ceramic bowl. Let the rice cool until it is not too hot to touch, but is still quite warm. Add the koji rice and mix in thoroughly. Cover the bowl lightly with a clean kitchen towel and set it aside for 6 to 12 hours, stirring occasionally and adding a pinch of salt with the second stirring. The time it takes to develop a rich fragrance and sweetness will depend on the temperature at which it rests. (If it is allowed to ferment too long, it will lose the sweetness and an alcoholic or sour quality may develop.) When the amazake tastes sweet, simmer for fifteen minutes to stop the active fermentation. It can then be processed in a blender until it is smooth, or enjoyed as is.

NOTE: To make a soothing drink, add a little extra water at this time. The drink can be served hot or cold, and flavored with a little vanilla extract or a few drops of juice squeezed from grated fresh ginger. This amazake beverage may be used as the liquid sweetener in almost any dessert or bread.

TEN-MINUTE
LEMONY PIE

hen it's too hot to use the oven, try making this unbaked "pie." Its lightness will please your guests as well. Makes 1 pie.

2 cups water

½ cup semolina ❖ *8 oz. soft-style tofu*

⅓ cup maple syrup ❖ *2 tablespoons lemon juice*

1 teaspoon almond extract ❖ *pinch sea salt*

½ cup chopped, roasted walnuts

Bring the water to boil in a saucepan and add the semolina, stirring rapidly to avoid lumps. Reduce heat and simmer for 2 to 3 minutes. Crumble the tofu into a blender or suribachi, and add the maple syrup, lemon juice, almond extract, and sea salt. Purée until smooth. Add the tofu mixture to the semolina, continuing to simmer and stir the entire mixture until it is well blended. Remove from the heat.

Lightly oil a glass pie plate, or a ceramic or enameled baking dish. Sprinkle the chopped nuts over the oiled surfaces, covering the bottom and sides of the pan with the nuts. Pour the pudding into this dish, spreading evenly. Allow the pie to cool before inverting it over a serving plate. To serve, cut it into wedges, as if cutting a pie.

ORANGE-ALMOND
PUDDING

a mazake-based, this is the ultimate pudding: sweet, creamy, and thick, with a hint of orange. And what is more, it is so mild that even a baby can digest it. Serves 4.

2 cups amazake (flavored with
½ teaspoon almond or vanilla extract)

6 oz. soymilk (plain or vanilla)

2 tablespoons kuzu dissolved in ½ cup water ❖ 1 orange

½ cup roasted, chopped almonds as a garnish

Pour the amazake and soymilk into a saucepan and bring to a boil over a medium heat. Dissolve the kuzu in the water. Add to the simmering amazake, stirring until thick. Lightly grate the orange rind, then extract the orange's juice. Add the orange juice and rind to amazake and simmer for about 2 minutes more. If the pudding is not thick, dissolve another teaspoon of kuzu in a small amount of cool water and add to the simmering pudding, stirring until thick. Garnish with almonds, or serve over Maria's Corncake (page 71) for a refreshing finish to a Mexican meal.

CORNMEAL PUDDING

innamon, raisins, and dried corn remind us of fall, but this pudding can easily serve as a light summer breakfast as well. Serves 8-10.

2 cups cornmeal ❖ *8 cups apple juice*

lightly grated rind of ½ lemon ❖ *pinch of sea salt*

1 cinnamon stick or 2 pinches cinnamon powder

½ cup currants or raisins

¼ cup tahini (optional)

toasted sunflower seeds, for garnish

Toast the cornmeal in a dry skillet over a low heat, stirring constantly until golden and fragrant. When it is cool, combine it with 4 cups of the apple juice.

Bring the remaining 4 cups apple juice to a simmer over medium-low heat and add the cornmeal mixture and the next 5 ingredients. Cover and let simmer over a low heat for 1 hour. Stir occasionally and use a heat diffuser under the pot to prevent scorching.

Serve the pudding hot, or pour it into a mold and chill it. To serve the chilled pudding, slice it and garnish with toasted sunflower seeds.

BREAD PUDDING

A hearty old-fashioned favorite, bread pudding is a delightfully efficient way to use up bread that shouldn't go to waste. Serves 4-5.

¼ cup raisins

2½ to 3 cups apple juice

4 cups stale bread, cubed

⅓ cup liquid sweetener
(maple syrup, barley malt syrup, or rice malt syrup)

1 egg, beaten ❖ cinnamon

Simmer the raisins in apple juice to cover, until they are plump. Drain the raisins and set them aside. Place the bread cubes in a bowl and pour measured juice and the sweetener over them. Let the bread stand for several hours, covered with the juice, until it is well soaked and very soft. Add more juice as needed to soften the bread cubes. Break up the cubes with a wooden spoon or masher. Mix in the beaten egg, the raisins, and a dash of cinnamon.

Pour the mixture into a baking dish, cover it and bake at 350° F for 30 minutes. Remove the cover for the last 5 minutes if a top crust is desired.

KHEER
(RICE PUDDING)

his richly elegant rice pudding, derived from India, provides a pleasingly aromatic variation on a favorite dessert theme. Serves 8-10.

1 cup brown or white basmati rice

water ❖ pinch sea salt

2 cups almonds, blanched

3 to 4 cups plain soymilk ❖ ¼ cup maple syrup

¼ teaspoon each cinnamon, cardamom, and clove powder or 1 cinnamon stick, 3 green cardamoms, and 6 cloves with the round tops removed

few strands saffron ❖ 1 handful seedless raisins

1 handful cashews or almonds

Wash the rice by rinsing it in several changes of water. Combine the rice with 2 cups water and salt and bring to a boil. Lower the flame, cover and simmer for 20 to 30 minutes or until the rice is soft and the water has been absorbed.

Blanch the almonds by dropping them into a pot of boiling water. Boil for 1 minute. Drain, and rinse with cold water. Remove the loosened almond skins. Blend the almonds with a cup of water until they are of a liquid consistency. Add the blended almonds and the soymilk to the rice and cook for 10 to 15 minutes. Stir to remove any lumps. You may have to add more soymilk or water. Add the remaining ingredients and simmer for ½ hour more. Adjust the seasonings. Serve warm or chilled.

RICE A L'AMANDE

In Norway, Sweden, and Denmark, an almond is "hidden" in this dish. The lucky one who finds it gets the "almond present," usually a little marzipan figure (page 111). Serves 8-10.

½ cup whole almonds

1½ cups water ❖ *¼ teaspoon sea salt*

2 teaspoons agar flakes ❖ *4 tablespoons rice malt syrup*

1 cup soft tofu ❖ *½ cup almond butter* ❖ *vanilla extract*

3 cups cooked brown rice

Scald the almonds, peel them, and chop all except 10 of them. Roast the chopped almonds in a dry skillet over medium-low heat, stirring constantly. Remove the almonds from the heat when they are just golden.

Bring the water to a boil and add the salt, agar, and rice malt syrup. Cook for 10 minutes. Crumble the tofu into this mixture and add the almond butter. Cook for a few minutes, then purée the tofu and almond butter mixture in a blender, adding a dash of vanilla. Combine it with the rice, 1 whole almond, and the roasted chopped almonds. Set it aside to cool (it will become more firm during this time) then decorate the top with the last 9 almonds. Serve with Cherry Sauce (page 97).

APPLE KANTEN

*K*anten, or agar, makes a light and refreshing gelatin that does not require refrigeration in order to set. Kanten can be made with any fruit or vegetable juice. Serves 4.

1 bar kanten or 2 tablespoons agar flakes

3 cups apple juice ❖ *pinch sea salt*

2 tablespoons kuzu dissolved in ¼ cup cold water

Rinse the kanten bar under cold water and squeeze it dry. Place the apple juice and the salt in a saucepan and shred the kanten into it. If you use the agar flakes, simply sprinkle them over the surface of the juice. They do not require rinsing. Bring the kanten and juice to a simmer over a medium heat. Continue to simmer for 3 to 4 minutes, stirring occasionally until the kanten is dissolved. Dissolve the kuzu in ¼ cup cold water and stir it into the juice mixture, continuing to stir the hot juice until it has become thick and clear.

Rinse a mold or bowl with cold water and pour in the hot kanten. Set it aside, uncovered, and chill until firm, about 1 to 2 hours.

VARIATION

Use any combination of fresh, seasonal fruits to dress up this simple dessert. Simply place the cut fruit in the mold and pour the hot kanten mixture over it, then cool.

STRAWBERRY MOUSSE

E njoy a light, healthful mousse
made with the season's first berries; you won't even miss the heavier cream
version. Serves 6-8.

4½ cups apple juice

1 bar kanten, or 2 tablespoons agar flakes

2 tablespoons tahini

1 cup sliced strawberries

8 whole fresh strawberries, for garnish

chopped, roasted nuts, for garnish

Rinse the kanten bar under cold water and squeeze it dry. Shred the bar, or
sprinkle the flakes, into a saucepan containing 4 cups cold apple juice. Bring to a
simmer without stirring. Simmer for 3 to 4 minutes, stirring occasionally. Blend
the tahini and ½ cup cold apple juice in a suribachi or blender.

Remove the kanten mixture from the heat, add the tahini mixture, and fold in the
strawberries. Pour the mousse into individual serving dishes that have been
rinsed with cold water. Chill for 1 to 2 hours or until firm. Garnish each serving
with a whole fresh strawberry and chopped roasted nuts.

MOCHA PARFAIT

or a two-toned parfait in a tall glass, alternate layers of Mocha Parfait with layers of almond or vanilla-flavored amazake pudding (page 20). Serves 6.

2 bars kanten
(or 4 tablespoons agar flakes)

2 cups apple juice
(or 2 cups water sweetened to taste with maple syrup)

2 cups grain coffee, instant or brewed ❖ *1 vanilla bean, split*

pinch sea salt ❖ *¼ to ½ cup tahini, to taste*

sliced, roasted almonds, for garnish

cinnamon

Rinse the kanten bars under cool water until soft. Combine the juice, grain coffee, vanilla bean, and salt in a saucepan. Shred the kanten bars into this mixture. If using agar flakes, simply sprinkle them over the liquids — they do not require rinsing. Bring the mixture to a boil, reduce the heat to medium-low, and simmer for 12 to 15 minutes, stirring occasionally.

Remove the vanilla bean and set the mixture aside. It will thicken slightly as it cools. Combine this mixture with the tahini in a blender or suribachi, and process until it is creamy. Pour into parfait or wine glasses, garnish with sliced almonds, and chill. Sprinkle lightly with cinnamon before serving.

3

PASTRIES

PEACH CRUMB

*T*he aroma of juicy, ripe peaches bubbling under a maple crumb topping will bring hungry tasters into the kitchen, eager for a slice of summer's bounty. Serves 6-8.

FILLING

10 ripe peaches ❖ *2 tablespoons barley malt syrup*

¼ teaspoon sea salt ❖ *1 teaspoon vanilla extract* ❖ *½ teaspoon cinnamon*

2 tablespoons arrowroot powder (do not use kuzu)

Halve the peaches and remove their pits. Slice each peach into 4 or 6 pieces, then combine them with the remaining ingredients, mixing lightly but thoroughly. Spread the filling out on a lightly oiled baking pan.

TOPPING

2½ cups whole wheat pastry flour

½ teaspoon sea salt ❖ *½ teaspoon cinnamon*

½ cup maple or barley malt syrup ❖ *¼ cup corn oil*

Preheat the oven to 325° F. Mix the dry ingredients. Mix the liquid ingredients. Add the liquids to the flour mixture and gently rub all together with your hands until mixture feels sandy. Crumble the topping over the peaches, then cover with foil. Bake for 30 minutes at 325° F, remove foil, and continue to bake for 5 to 10 minutes more. Peach Crumb should be served at room temperature.

DATE BARS

Hearty rolled oats, combined with the delicate sweetness of coconut, maple syrup, and dates, create a rich bar that will satisfy sweet-tooth cravings. A little bit goes a long way. Makes 16 bars.

TOPPING

1½ cups rolled oats

1 cup whole wheat pastry flour ❖ *⅓ cup flaked, unsweetened coconut*

¼ cup chopped, roasted walnuts ❖ *¼ teaspoon sea salt* ❖ *¼ cup corn oil*

⅓ cup maple syrup (optional) ❖ *1 teaspoon vanilla extract*

Preheat the oven to 350° F. Combine the oats, flour, coconut, walnuts, and salt in a bowl. Mix in the oil, then add the syrup and vanilla. Spread the topping on a cookie sheet and bake for 5 to 7 minutes. Set it aside to cool.

FILLING

3 cups pitted dates

1 to 1½ cups water ❖ *¼ teaspoon sea salt*

Purée the dates, water, and salt together in a blender. Spread one-third of the topping in a lightly oiled baking dish. Add the date, smoothing it over the topping with a spatula. Sprinkle the remaining topping over the date filling and press it down well. Cover with foil and bake for 30 minutes. Cut into squares when it has cooled thoroughly.

CHERRY CRISP

he sweet and tart flavors of fresh ripe cherries highlight this summertime dessert, the perfect finale to a light warm-weather meal. Serves 4-5.

FILLING

2 cups ripe cherries ❖ *1 ¼ cups water*

¼ teaspoon sea salt ❖ *2 tablespoons maple syrup*

2 tablespoons arrowroot powder, dissolved in ¼ cup water

juice of ½ lemon

Pit the cherries and place them in a heavy saucepan with the water, salt, and syrup. Bring to a boil. Dilute the arrowroot in the quarter cup of water and stir it into the cherries. Cover and simmer for 5 minutes. Remove from the heat, set aside for 5 minutes, then add the lemon juice.

TOPPING

6 cups oat flour ❖ *½ teaspoon sea salt*

⅔ cup corn oil ❖ *⅓ cup maple syrup* ❖ *⅔ tablespoon water*

1 teaspoon vanilla

Oat flour can be made quickly from whole oats or rolled oats. To improve their flavor, pan-roast the oats for 4 to 5 minutes before grinding or blending.

Preheat the oven to 350° F. Combine the flour and sea salt and mix well. Add the oil, and mix in lightly with a fork. Mix in the syrup, then add the water and vanilla, and continue mixing lightly until the topping becomes crumbly.

Spread the topping evenly over a baking sheet and bake for 8 to 10 minutes. After the mixture has been in the oven for 5 minutes, stir it lightly with a spatula. Place one-third of the crumbs in a baking dish, pour in one-third of the cherry filling, and repeat the process, ending with a layer of crumbs. Cover and bake for 25 to 30 minutes at 325° F. Uncover for the last 5 minutes of baking time.

hen you want an exotic dessert, try this unusual tart. Ground filberts create a delicate pressed crust. Seedless grapes and kiwi fruit lend freshness to a lightly sweetened, gelled filling. Serves 8-10.

CRUST

¼ cup corn oil

¼ cup water ❖ *pinch of sea salt*

¼ cup rice malt syrup or barley malt syrup

½ teaspoon vanilla extract

1 cup filberts or almonds, toasted and ground fine

1 cup whole wheat pastry flour ❖ *¼ cup rice flour or graham flour*

NOTE: After toasting the filberts, rub them between your hands to remove skins.

Combine the corn oil, water, salt, sweetener, and vanilla extract in a small pan and heat, stirring until smooth. Mix the ground nuts and the flours in a bowl and add the liquid ingredients. When the dough is mixed, press it into a tart pan. Bake at 400° F for 15 to 20 minutes. Set aside to cool.

NOTE: An ideal type of pan to use is the classic French tart pan, 10½ inches in diameter, 1 inch high, with fluted sides and a removable bottom.

FILLING

2 small ripe kiwi fruits, peeled and sliced into rounds

1½ pounds green or red seedless grapes

2⅓ cups apple juice ❖ 2 tablespoons agar flakes

*2 to 3 tablespoons rice malt syrup or
barley malt syrup (optional)*

*4 tablespoons arrowroot powder,
dissolved in ¼ cup water*

Wash the grapes and remove them from their stems. On the pie crust, arrange an outer circle of grapes and an inner circle of kiwi rounds. Fill the center with grapes. Set aside.

Place the apple juice, agar, and sweetener into a 2½ quart pan. Bring to a boil and simmer for 10 minutes. Dissolve the arrowroot in ¼ cup water and add to the simmering liquid. Stir until the glaze is well thickened. Pour the hot glaze over the fruit. Let the tart and glaze cool before cutting.

ALMOND TORTE
WITH RASPBERRY FILLING

his rich torte, created by natural foods chef Mary Estella, adds a touch of old-world class to a festive occasion. Apricot purée or other jams may be used in place of raspberry jam. Serves 8-10.

1 cup almonds ❖ 1 cup rolled oats

1 cup whole wheat pastry flour ❖ pinch sea salt

½ cup maple syrup ❖ ½ cup corn oil ❖ 4 ounces raspberry jam

Preheat the oven to 300° F. Roast the almonds and the oats in separate, flat baking pans by baking for 10 to 15 minutes (for the almonds) and 5 to 10 minutes (for the oats).

Chop the almonds coarsely and grind them to a crumbly consistency in a blender or nut grinder. In a blender, grind the oats to a finer, powdery flour. Combine the oat flour, ground almonds, whole wheat pastry flour, pinch of sea salt, and cinnamon in a mixing bowl. Beat the maple syrup and the corn oil together. Form a well in the dry ingredients, add the syrup and corn oil, and mix.

Lightly oil a round baking dish or 9-inch pie pan. Gently press ⅔ of the dough into this dish. Spread the jam evenly over the dough with a spatula. With the remaining dough, form small 1-inch balls and gently flatten them into discs the size of a quarter. Arrange the discs in two circles on the raspberry-covered dough, leaving a 1-inch space between the discs and placing one disc in the center of the raspberry filling.

Bake at 350° F for 15 to 20 minutes, or until the crust is golden.

TOFU
CHEESECAKE

his delicious "cheesecake" is a lighter, non-dairy relative of a rich and heavy old favorite. Spread fresh fruit sauce over the top. Serves 6-8.

CRUST

2 cups of your favorite granola

apple juice

Preheat the oven to 350° F. Put the granola in a blender and blend into fine crumbs. In a large bowl, add just enough apple juice to the granola to make it stick together. Oil a 9-inch spring-form pan and press the crust into the bottom of the pan. Bake for 10 minutes. Set aside to cool.

FILLING

4 cakes tofu ❖ *4-8 tablespoons maple syrup*

⅓ cup tahini ❖ *1 teaspoon vanilla extract* ❖ *2 teaspoons lemon juice*

½ teaspoon sea salt

Press the tofu to remove excess liquid. Put it into a blender with the remaining ingredients and process until creamy. Pour the filling into the baked crust and bake at 325° F for 30 minutes. When the center of the tofu is firm, turn off the heat and let the cake remain in the oven for another 30 minutes. Remove from the oven and let it rest for at least 6 hours before removing it from the pan. The cake should be set aside in a cool place for 2 to 4 days to allow its full flavor to develop.

DREAM PUFFS

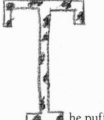

he puffs that dreams are made of —
filled with lemon- and vanilla-flavored amazake and topped with carob sauce.
Combine puffs, filling, and sauce just before serving. Makes 20 Puffs.

FILLING

5 cups thick amazake (page 20)

1 tablespoon agar flakes (not agar powder or kanten bar)

1 tablespoon lightly grated lemon rind

1 teaspoon vanilla extract

Blend the amazake in a blender or food mill. Heat 2 cups of the amazake to
boiling and add the agar flakes. Simmer for 5 minutes. Mix well with the
remaining amazake, and add lemon rind and vanilla. Chill.

PUFFS

¼ cup corn oil ❖ *½ cup water*

½ cup whole wheat flour or unbleached white flour

2 eggs

Preheat the oven to 400° F. Add the oil to the water and bring to a low boil. Add
the flour all at once, stirring quickly to form a ball of dough in the center of the
pot. Remove from the heat and add the eggs one at a time, beating well after each
addition. The mixture should be stiff.

Drop by tablespoons onto a lightly oiled cookie sheet and bake for 10 minutes. Reduce the heat to 300° F, and continue to bake the puffs for 25 minutes more. Remove the puffs from the oven and set them aside to cool. Slice off the tops and remove any wet dough from the insides. Fill with the cool amazake just before serving. Top each filled puff with 1 to 2 teaspoons carob sauce.

CAROB SAUCE

2 tablespoons tahini

¼ cup rice malt syrup

4 tablespoons roasted carob powder

2 tablespoons arrowroot, dissolved in ¼ cup water

Heat the tahini, rice malt syrup, and carob in a saucepan. Dissolve the arrowroot powder in the water and add it to the mixture. Stir until it thickens. Use 1 to 2 teaspoons of sauce for each puff.

43

4

PIES

BASIC ROLLED CRUST

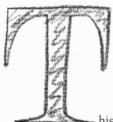his versatile crust recipe is quick and easy. Makes two single-crusted pies or one double-crusted pie.

1½ cups unbleached white flour

1½ cups whole wheat pastry flour ❖ *½ teaspoon sea salt*

⅓-½ cup corn oil ❖ *½ cup (approximately) ice-cold water*

Fluff the flours and salt together with a fork. Add oil and use a fork or your fingers to combine it with the flours until the mixture is crumbly but not oily. Add water one spoonful at a time, quickly mixing a soft and workable dough. If you are not using the dough immediately, wrap it in waxed paper and chill.

Rolling out the dough between layers of waxed paper prevents the dough from becoming dry and heavy with extra flour. Dampen your work surface to prevent the paper from sliding, and lay out a large piece of waxed paper. Place half of the pie dough on the paper and flatten it a little with your hand. Cover the dough with another large sheet of waxed paper. Roll the dough thinly and evenly, stroking outward from the center. Peel off the top layer of paper, invert the dough over a pie plate, and peel away the remaining paper. Pat the dough onto the pie plate, and prick it in several places with a fork. Fill the pie shell.

Use the same method to roll out the top crust slightly thinner than the bottom crust, using two fresh pieces of waxed paper. Remove the top piece of paper and pick the rolled dough up with the bottom layer of paper to invert it over the filled pie. Remove the paper. Trim and flute the edges and make a few decorative slashes in the top crust to allow steam to escape. Bake as directed for recipe.

BASIC PRESSED CRUST

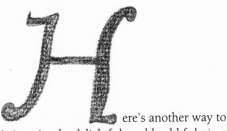

ere's another way to begin your favorite pies. This is a simple, delightful, and healthful pie crust especially good for vegetable pies. Makes one single-crust pie shell.

1 cup whole wheat pastry flour

1 cup rolled oats

¼ teaspoon sea salt

⅓ cup corn oil

2 to 3 tablespoons water

Combine the flour, oats, and salt in a mixing bowl. Add the oil and work into flour with a fork. Add water, mix well, and let sit 2-3 minutes. Press the mixture into a pie plate to a thickness of ¼ inch. Prebake for 10 minutes at 350° F.

VARIATION

Crumble the following crunchy topping over your favorite puddings and cooked fruit. Substitute maple syrup for the water, and add 1 to 2 teaspoons vanilla extract. Mix lightly and spread the topping mixture on a baking sheet. Bake at 350° F for no more than 8 to 10 minutes.

DUTCH APPLE PIE

The addition of raisins and almonds to apple pie is a European variation on a beloved American theme. Makes one double-crusted pie.

1 recipe Basic Rolled Crust

8 apples (McIntosh or Cortland) ❖ *¼ teaspoon sea salt*

½ cup apple butter ❖ *⅓ cup combined raisins and chopped almonds*

⅓ cup arrowroot powder

Core apples and thinly slice. Combine with salt, apple butter, and the raisin-almond mixture. Sprinkle the arrowroot powder over the apples and toss lightly to coat evenly. Preheat the oven to 450° F.

Divide a two-crust pie dough into two balls, one slightly larger than the other. Roll the larger ball into a circle and trim the edges. Fold the dough in half, place in a lightly oiled pie plate, and open it out. The edges of the dough should extend over the rim of the plate.

Fill the pie shell. Repeat the rolling process for the top crust then lay the top over the filling. Fold the edges of the top crust under the edges of the bottom crust and flute the edges by hand, or use a fork to seal the crusts together by pressing it along the rim of the pie plate. Prick the top crust to allow steam to escape.

Bake at 450° F for 15 minutes, then reduce the heat to 350° F and bake for 30 minutes more until the top crust is lightly browned.

BLUEBERRY PIE

When the juice bubbles up through the top crust, you'll be glad you picked all those blueberries. Notice that the recipe yields two double-crusted pies.

2 recipes Basic Rolled Crust

2 pints fresh (or unsweetened frozen) blueberries

1 to 1¼ cups barley malt syrup ❖ *juice of 1 lemon*

2 teaspoons vanilla extract ❖ *½ teaspoon sea salt*

3 tablespoons arrowroot powder (do not use kuzu)

Wash the berries and remove their stems. Combine all ingredients and mix them gently but thoroughly.

Prepare the pie dough for two double-crusted pies. Roll out the bottom crusts and line the pie plates with them. Fill each with half of the blueberry mixture. Roll out the top crusts thinner than the bottom crusts. Seal and flute the edges and make a few decorative slashes in the top crusts to allow steam to escape. Bake at 375° F for 45 minutes.

Allow the pies to cool completely before serving.

LEMON CHIFFON PIE

This elegant dessert calls for a pre-baked single crust. You need only prepare the filling, which can also be done in advance of serving. Then, enjoy the pie and your guests. Makes one single-crusted pie.

½ recipe Basic Rolled Crust (single crust)

1½ cups water ❖ 2 tablespoons arrowroot powder

2 tablespoons whole wheat pastry flour ❖ ⅓ cup maple syrup

2 eggs, separated ❖ juice of 1 to 2 lemons ❖ grated rind of ½ lemon

2 tablespoons maple syrup

Prebake one pie shell for a single-crusted pie.

Boil the water in the top of a double boiler or in a heavy saucepan. Dilute the arrowroot and the flour in ⅓ cup syrup and whisk into the boiling water, stirring until thick. Reduce the heat to low, cover the pot, and simmer for 3 to 4 minutes.

Beat together the egg yolks and 1 teaspoon water. Remove the filling from the heat and set it aside for a few minutes to cool. Beat in the egg yolks slowly so they do not cook. Return the filling to a low heat for 5 minutes, then add the lemon juice and the rind. Turn the mixture out into a bowl and cover with a sheet of waxed paper. Set it aside to cool to room temperature.

Beat the egg whites until stiff. Continue beating them while threading in 2 tablespoons maple syrup. Gently fold the egg whites into the lemon filling. Pour the completed filling into the prebaked pie shell and chill for at least 1 hour before serving.

GINGER PEACH PIE

a n exotic version of the peach pie, with a hint of ginger to flavor the syrup. Partially cooked peaches means that this summertime pie needs to be baked only for twenty minutes. Makes one double-crusted pie.

1 recipe Basic Rolled Crust

2 to 3 pounds fresh peaches ❖ 1 tablespoon corn oil

¼ cup maple syrup or rice malt syrup

pinch sea salt ❖ 1 tablespoon grated fresh ginger

1 tablespoon whole wheat pastry flour

Wash and slice the peaches. Heat the oil in a pot over a medium heat, add the peaches, and sauté them very briefly. Add the syrup and a pinch of salt. Lower the heat and cook the peaches until they are about halfway tender, stirring occasionally. Mix in the grated ginger, then sprinkle the flour over the surface and mix in carefully, to thicken the cooking juices. Remove the pot from the heat.

Preheat the oven to 450° F.

Prepare the dough for one double-crust pie. Fill the pie and add the top crust. Seal and flute the edges and make a few slashes in the top crust to allow excess steam to escape. Bake for 20 minutes or until the pie is golden and the filling is bubbling through the slashes in the top crust. Let the pie cool completely before serving.

SQUASH PIE

Hearty squash pie is a traditional alternative to pumpkin in the fall and winter. Made with less or no sweetener it can be served with the main course as a vegetable pie. Makes one single-crusted pie.

½ recipe Basic Rolled Crust (single-crust shell)

1 medium buttercup or butternut squash

½ cup water ❖ *¼ teaspoon sea salt*

½ teaspoon cinnamon ❖ *⅓ cup maple syrup*

2 eggs, separated

Cut the squash into large chunks and remove the skin, seeds, and strings. Place the squash in a pressure cooker with the water, salt, and cinnamon. Bring to pressure, reduce heat to low, and process for 10 minutes.

NOTE: If boiling, use ¾ to 1 cup water in a heavy pot with a tight-fitting lid and cook for 20 to 30 minutes or until the squash is very tender.

Remove the pot from the heat. Place the pressure cooker under running cold water to reduce pressure to normal. Drain the squash and let it cool. Preheat the oven to 350° F.

Prepare a single-crusted pie shell and prebake it for 10 minutes. Purée the squash in a blender or food mill. Beat in the syrup and egg yolks. Fold in the stiffly beaten egg whites and pour the filling into the prebaked shell. Bake at 350° F for 30 to 35 minutes. Allow the pie to cool thoroughly before slicing.

MINCE NO-MEAT PIE

This dark and fruity holiday pie is one that is best served in small slices, but you can expect requests for seconds. Makes one double-crusted pie.

1 recipe Basic Rolled Crust

2 cups raisins (or 1 cup raisins, 1 cup currants, prunes, or pears), soaked overnight in 3 cups apple juice

4 cups apples (peeled, cored, and cut into chunks)

2 tablespoons rice or barley miso

½ tablespoon cinnamon and/or allspice

2 tablespoons kuzu or arrowroot powder dissolved in 2 tablespoons water

1 tablespoon lightly grated orange peel

1 tablespoon orange juice

½ cup walnuts, chopped

Prepare the pie dough and refrigerate it. In a heavy uncovered pot, cook the apples and dried fruit and juice over a medium heat for 1 hour. Remove ½ cup cooking liquid. Add miso to it and purée. Add puréed miso to pot and cook for 15 minutes more. Add the spices and mix well.

Dissolve the kuzu in the water and add it to the fruit. Add the orange peel and orange juice to the hot fruit, stirring constantly as the sauce thickens and becomes clear. Mix in the walnuts. Set aside to cool while crusts are prepared.

Fill the bottom crust. Use a lattice-weave top crust to make this pie especially attractive, or cover with a full top crust. Press the edges together and flute, so the edges are well sealed. If a full top crust is used, cut decorative slashes and bake at 375° F for 30 to 40 minutes. Allow the pie to cool before serving.

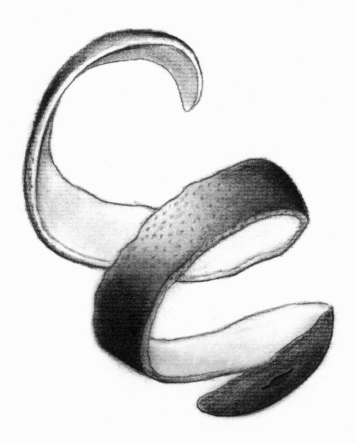

5

COOKIES

COOKIE CUTTER
COOKIES

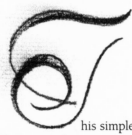

his simple recipe is for a cookie dough that will be chilled, rolled out, and cut into festive shapes. Children, of course, love to press the cookie cutters into the dough. Makes about two dozen cookies.

2½ cups whole wheat pastry flour

1 cup nut meal

½ teaspoon sea salt

1 teaspoon lemon rind

¼ cup corn oil

⅓ cup maple syrup

½ cup water

Combine the flour, nut meal, salt, and lemon rind in a mixing bowl. Mix in the oil, then the syrup. Slowly add the water to form a dough that gathers into a ball. Chill for 1 hour. Preheat the oven to 350° F. Divide the dough in half and roll out onto a lightly floured surface, ¼ inch thick. Cut with cookie cutters and bake for 12 to 15 minutes on a lightly oiled baking sheet.

MICHAEL'S
PEANUT BUTTER GEMS

When Michael makes peanut butter cookies, he doesn't fool around. Children can easily help to make, and love to eat, these nutty little gems. Makes 40 2-inch cookies.

1 pound peanut butter ❖ *⅔ cup corn oil*

1 cup maple syrup (or half barley malt syrup and half maple syrup)

1 teaspoon vanilla extract

3 cups sifted whole wheat pastry flour

½ teaspoon sea salt

Preheat the oven to 350° F. Cream the first four ingredients together until smooth. Sift together flour and salt. Gradually add the sifted flour, mixing well. Form 2-inch balls. Place them on a lightly oiled cookie sheet and flatten them slightly. Bake the cookies for 10 minutes or just until golden. Allow the cookies to cool for 5 minutes before removing to a rack to cool thoroughly.

ALL-TIME FAVORITE
MAPLE WALNUT COOKIES

W hat gives these cookies their claim to fame? A generous amount of maple syrup and walnuts has turned them into celebrities, and they truly are irresistible. Yields 36 2-inch cookies.

1½ cups rolled oats

3 cups whole wheat pastry flour

½ teaspoon sea salt ❖ *½ cup corn oil* ❖ *1 cup maple syrup*

1 tablespoon vanilla ❖ *1½ cups roasted walnuts*

⅓-2 cups water

Preheat oven to 350°F. In a large bowl, mix the oats, flour, and salt followed by the oil, syrup, vanilla, walnuts, and water. The amount of water you use — from ⅓ to 2 cups — will determine the cookies' texture and firmness. A small amount of water will make a more crisp cookie. More water will make it soft and chewy. In addition, handground flours or oats absorb about 25 percent more liquid than finely ground commercially prepared flours. When ingredients are well mixed, drop onto a lightly oiled cookie sheet by the spoonful, pressing the dough lightly. Bake for 18-20 minutes.

THE ULTIMATE
ALMOND COOKIE

round almonds are the foundation of these flourless, oil-free cookies. The nuts impart a delicate flavor and texture and the malt syrup gives them a subtle sweetness. Makes 18 cookies.

3 cups almonds

¼ to ½ cup apple juice ❖ *juice of 1 orange*

1 teaspoon vanilla extract ❖ *½ teaspoon cinnamon*

1 cup rice malt syrup or barley malt syrup

½ teaspoon sea salt

Preheat the oven to 325° F. Grind the almonds in a blender to make almond meal. Add enough apple juice to make a smooth paste. Combine the almond paste with remaining ingredients. Drop by tablespoons onto a well-oiled baking sheet and press each cookie lightly with a fork.

Bake on a high rack for 10 minutes or just until the cookies are golden. Watch these cookies closely — they are delicate and may burn easily.

RASPBERRY DROP COOKIES

A generous dollop of raspberry jam turns these cookies into jewels; but if you don't have raspberry on hand, use peach jam, orange marmalade, or apple cider jelly. Makes 10 to 12 large cookies.

3 cups whole wheat pastry flour

½ teaspoon sea salt ❖ *½ teaspoon cinnamon*

1 cup barley malt syrup ❖ *½ cup maple syrup* ❖ *½ cup corn oil*

1 teaspoon vanilla extract

raspberry jam

Mix the dry ingredients together. Mix the liquid ingredients (except the jam) and combine them with the dry, stirring lightly to just mix — don't knead or overwork, or the cookies may be tough. Roll the dough into balls and place on a lightly oiled baking sheet. Lightly moisten the palm of your hand and press down gently on each cookie. Make an indentation with your thumb and fill the space with the raspberry jam. Before baking, refrigerate the formed cookies for 60 minutes or until thoroughly chilled.

Bake at 325° F for 25 minutes. Remove the cookies from the oven and allow them to remain on the tray until they are cool. The heat from the cookie sheet will finish the baking.

COCONUT MACAROONS

Tiny morsels of coconut, sweetened with amazake or maple syrup, are beautiful accompaniments to an afternoon cup of hot tea. Makes about 20 1-inch cookies.

1 cup shredded
unsweetened coconut

1 teaspoon vanilla extract ❖ *pinch sea salt*

amazake beverage or maple syrup (page 20)

1 to 3 egg whites (optional, but makes a lighter, fluffier cookie)

Preheat the oven to 250° F. Mix the coconut, vanilla, and salt with just enough amazake to make a thick paste. Beat the egg whites until stiff but not too dry. Fold the egg whites into the batter and drop by teaspoons onto an oiled baking sheet. Bake for 60 to 90 minutes or until lightly browned.

BISCOTTI AL ANICE
(ANISE COOKIES)

 eminiscent of afternoons in an Italian café, these anise-flavored half-moon cookies are homey and fancy at the same time. Makes 40 cookies.

¾ cup sliced almonds

2 teaspoons ground or whole anise, or ¼ teaspoon anise extract

½ cup sesame seeds ❖ 2 cups whole wheat pastry flour

1 teaspoon non-aluminum baking powder

½ cup barley malt syrup ❖ ⅓ cup corn oil ❖ ¼ cup water

Lightly toast ½ cup of the almonds, and set aside ¼ cup to be used as a garnish. Grind the anise. Grind the sesame seeds to a coarse meal or toast them and leave whole. Combine the first five ingredients. Mix the barley malt syrup, corn oil, and water until smooth. Combine the dry and wet ingredients and mix gently.

Oil a cookie sheet. Divide the dough in half. Form a ball with each half, then shape into a log, about 3 inches wide and ½ to 1 inch high, that will fit lengthwise on the cookie sheet. Gently press the remaining almonds into the top of the dough.

Bake at 350° F for 15 minutes, or until golden brown. Allow the roll to cool slightly, then cut it while it is still warm. Make the slices about 1 inch wide, cut at a 45 degree angle.

COCONUT JEWEL COOKIES

These cookies are chewy and delicious. The recipe doubles or triples well so make plenty for the holidays.

1 cup walnuts

1 cup flaked, unsweetened coconut

1 cup whole wheat pastry flour ❖ pinch sea salt

1 teaspoon non-aluminum baking powder (optional)

½ cup dates ❖ ¼ cup corn oil

1 orange (extract the juice and grate the rind)

water (to equal ½ cup when combined with orange juice)

¼ cup hot water

Preheat the oven to 350° F. Chop the walnuts and combine with dry ingredients. Pit and chop the dates and combine with the wet ingredients to make a smooth paste. If the dates are very dry, a little extra liquid may be needed. Add the wet ingredients to the dry, and mix well to form the cookie dough. Form balls 1 to 2 inches in diameter and place them on a lightly oiled cookie sheet. Flatten slightly and garnish with walnut halves. Bake for 12 to 15 minutes or until just golden.

VARIATION

Omit the walnut garnish. Make a thumb print indentation, then fill it with orange marmalade or your favorite fruit preserve.

CAROB BROWNIES

Carob brownies are easy to prepare. The recipe can be doubled or tripled, making these confections ideal for parties and large gatherings. Makes 16 brownies.

2 eggs

1½ cups barley malt syrup

⅓ cup maple syrup ❖ *½ cup corn oil*

2 cups whole wheat pastry flour

1½ cups carob powder ❖ *1 teaspoon sea salt*

1½ cups roasted walnuts ❖ *1 teaspoon vanilla extract*

1 to 1½ cups water

Preheat the oven to 350° F. In a large mixing bowl, beat the eggs until they are light and frothy. Add the barley malt syrup, maple syrup, and oil, mixing well after each addition. Add the flour, carob, salt, walnuts, vanilla, and water, and mix to a smooth batter. Bake in a 7½ inch square pan for 20 to 25 minutes. This will make a chewy, moist brownie. For a lighter, cakier texture bake in an 8 inch by 10 inch pan for 15 to 20 minutes.

CAKES

VANILLA CAKE

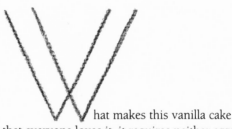

hat makes this vanilla cake so special? Besides the fact that everyone loves it, it requires neither eggs nor milk. Makes a 9-inch cake or 24 muffins.

2 ¼ cups whole wheat pastry flour

½ teaspoon sea salt ❖ *2 teaspoons non-aluminum baking powder*

½ cup corn oil ❖ *1 cup barley malt syrup or maple syrup*

1 tablespoon vanilla extract

1 cup water

Preheat the oven to 375° F. Sift the dry ingredients together. Combine the liquid ingredients, then slowly stir them into the flour mixture. Pour the batter into an oiled cake pan or 24 muffin tins. Bake for 30 minutes or until a toothpick inserted into the center comes out dry. Place on a rack to cool before cutting.

VARIATIONS

For *Lemon-Ginger Cake*, add 1 tablespoon lemon juice, 1 teaspoon grated lemon rind, and ½ teaspoon juice squeezed from fresh grated ginger. Substitute baking soda for baking powder.

For *Gingerbread*, substitute cooled, prepared grain coffee for the water, and add ½ teaspoon cinnamon, ½ teaspoon allspice, and 1 teaspoon juice squeezed from fresh grated ginger.

MARIA'S CORNCAKE

this light, sweet cake, suitable for a "luncheon on the grass," can be baked in a small cake pan or in muffin tins. Makes one 9-inch cake or 24 muffins.

1 cup whole wheat pastry flour

1 cup cornmeal ❖ *pinch sea salt*

1 tablespoon non-aluminum baking powder

1 cup water ❖ *¼ cup corn oil*

¼ cup maple syrup

Preheat the oven to 375° F. Sift together the flour, cornmeal, salt, and baking powder, then add the bran sifted from the flour back into the bowl. Combine the liquid ingredients and mix well. Add the liquid to the dry ingredients and mix gently. Pour the batter into a small oiled cake pan, or use muffin tins and fill to ⅔ capacity. Bake for 15 minutes or until the cake is golden brown.

Slice and serve the cake while it is still warm.

SERVING SUGGESTIONS

Slice each piece of cake in half, and top with Orange-Almond Pudding (page 23), fresh strawberries and roasted almonds. Try raspberries or blueberries in season.

STEPHEN'S
LAYERED CARROT CAKE

 sweet and nutritious carrot cake, topped with a lemony apple glaze. It is perfect for birthday parties or any special celebration. Makes a double-layered round cake.

1 cup chopped walnuts (or other nuts of your choice)

3½ cups whole wheat pastry flour ❖ *1 teaspoon sea salt*

1 teaspoon cinnamon ❖ *1 tablespoon non-aluminum baking powder*

1 cup corn oil ❖ *½ cup apple juice*

2 cups maple syrup ❖ *3 carrots, grated*

2 teaspoons grated fresh ginger

Preheat the oven to 350° F. Spread the nuts on a cookie sheet and place them in the oven for 10 minutes or until fragrant. Chop the nuts and set them aside.

Sift the dry ingredients together. Combine the liquid ingredients and add them to the dry ingredients. Add the grated carrots and ginger. Pour the batter into two oiled layer pans and bake for 30 to 40 minutes or until a knife inserted into the center of the cake comes out clean. Cool the cakes on a rack.

GLAZE

4 lemons (use juice from 2, and lightly grated rind of 4)

2 cups apple juice ❖ pinch sea salt

2 tablespoons arrowroot powder dissolved in ½ cup water

Combine the lemon rind, lemon juice, apple juice, and salt in a saucepan and bring to a simmer over medium-low heat. Combine the arrowroot and water and stir it into the simmering liquid. Cook and stir for 2 minutes, until the mixture is thick. Set aside to cool.

Spread the glaze over one layer of the cake. Place the second layer on top, sprinkle the chopped nuts over it, and spread the remaining glaze over the top.

ractically a pudding, this dense, moist cake will warm your favorite guests throughout the winter season. Makes a 9-inch round cake.

4 cups raisins

3 cups apple juice

3 cups whole wheat pastry flour

1 cup chopped almonds or walnuts ❖ *¼ cup corn oil*

1 teaspoon grated lemon rind ❖ *2 teaspoons lemon juice*

½ teaspoon sea salt ❖ *2 teaspoons vanilla extract*

2 tablespoons miso ❖ *4 cups apple chunks*

Preheat the oven to 325° F. Combine the raisins and apple juice in a large saucepan and simmer over a medium-low heat for 30 to 40 minutes. Set aside to cool. Roast the flour in a dry skillet over medium-low heat until it is fragrant, stirring constantly. Set aside. Spread the nuts on a cookie sheet and roast in the oven for 10 to 15 minutes or until fragrant. Chop the nuts and set them aside.

Combine the oil, lemon rind and juice, salt, vanilla, and miso with the raisins and apple juice. Sift the flour into this mixture and stir until smooth. Fold in the chopped nuts and apple chunks. Pour the batter into an oiled and floured cake pan, cover with foil, and bake for 40 minutes. Uncover the cake and bake it for about 20 minutes more, or until the cake is set.

POPPYSEED CAKE

T he delicate flavor of poppy seeds permeates this rich, moist cake. Blended tofu contributes to the full but light texture. Makes one 9-inch cake.

2 cups unbleached white flour

1 cup whole wheat pastry flour

1 tablespoon non-aluminum baking powder

¼ teaspoon sea salt ❖ ¼ teaspoon cinnamon

1 cup maple syrup ❖ ¾ cup corn oil ❖ ¼ cup tahini

¼ to 1 cup apple juice ❖ ¼ pound tofu

½ cup poppyseeds

Preheat the oven to 325° F. Sift the dry ingredients together. Place the wet ingredients, including the tofu, into a blender and process until smooth. Combine the wet and dry ingredients and add the poppyseeds. The mixture should be a thick, fluffy batter. Pour into an oiled cake pan and bake for 45 to 55 minutes. Place on a rack to cool. Ice with Currant Frosting (page 103).

STEAMED
COUSCOUS CAKE

oist and pudding-like, couscous cake flavored with ginger is a satisfying, yet not too heavy, winter dessert. Makes one large bundt cake.

1 cup raisins or currants

1 cup chopped dried apricots
(or other dried or fresh fruit of your choice)

6 cups apple juice ❖ *1 cup brown rice flour*

2 cups uncooked couscous ❖ *1 teaspoon cinnamon*

½ teaspoon powdered cloves ❖ *½ cup corn oil*

1 teaspoon juice squeezed from grated
fresh ginger or ½ teaspoon powdered ginger

shaved lemon rind, or jam, as garnish

Soak the fruit in the apple juice for 6 to 8 hours or overnight. Roast rice flour in a dry skillet over a medium-low heat, stirring until golden. Set aside to cool.

Mix together flour, couscous, cinnamon, and cloves. Using your hands, rub the oil and ginger juice into the dry ingredients. Heat the apple juice and fruit almost to boiling and add to the dry ingredients. Stir the batter gently until the couscous begins to expand and the batter becomes thick but still pourable.

Pour the batter into an unoiled *bundt* pan or mold and cover tightly with foil. Put 1½ inches of water in a pot large enough to hold the cake pan. Place the filled cake pan into the pot with water, and cover the pot. Make sure that no water or direct steam reaches the cake. Place the pot over a medium heat and let the cake steam for 30 minutes.

Allow the cake to cool before slicing. Garnish each serving with a small spoonful of jam, shaved lemon rind, or both.

ALTERNATE COOKING METHOD

The cake may also be baked at 325° F for 20 to 30 minutes in a mold or loaf pan, covered with foil.

GUINNESS
SPICE CAKE

spice cake which can double as a holiday fruitcake, this confection calls for real Guinness Stout to impart an old-world flavor. Yields 2 loaves.

5 cups whole wheat pastry flour

3 cups rolled oats ❖ *¼ teaspoon sea salt*

¼ teaspoon each of cinnamon, cloves, and allspice

½ cup sunflower or sesame oil

1½ cups raisins ❖ *1¼ cups walnuts, chopped*

1 cup barley malt syrup or rice malt syrup

3 12 oz. bottles Guinness Stout

NOTE: For a lighter cake, add 2 eggs and ¼ teaspoon
non-aluminum baking powder

Mix flour, oats, salt, and spices together. If you are using baking powder, add it in with the dry ingredients. Rub the oil in with your hands. Add the raisins and nuts, then the syrup. If you are using eggs, beat them separately and add them into the other ingredients. Add 18 to 24 ounces of the Guinness Stout, or enough to make a thick batter. Beat eggs and add, with baking powder, if desired.

Preheat the oven to 350° F. Pour the batter into two well-oiled standard-size loaf pans. Bake for 30 minutes, then reduce the oven heat to 325° F and continue to bake for 2½ to 3 hours, or until a knife inserted into the center of the cakes comes out clean.

Allow the cakes to cool and remove from the pans. Turn the cakes over and poke ¼-inch holes in the bottom of each. Spoon 6 ounces of Guinness over each cake. Set the cakes aside overnight to allow them to absorb the Guinness.

VARIATION

To produce a delicious fruitcake, wrap the cakes in foil and store at room temperature for several days before serving.

CRANBERRY-CORN MUFFINS

*T*art cranberries and sweet cornmeal — an irresistible New England combination enhanced by the taste of maple syrup. Makes 18 muffins.

1 cup cornmeal

2 cups whole wheat pastry flour

1 tablespoon non-aluminum baking powder

½ teaspoon cinnamon ❖ *pinch sea salt*

4 oz. soft tofu, or 2 eggs ❖ *½ cup maple syrup*

½ cup corn oil ❖ *¾ cup water*

¾ cup cranberries

Preheat the oven to 375° F. Mix the dry ingredients in a large bowl. Use a blender or electric mixer to purée the wet ingredients until smooth. Add the wet ingredients to the dry — do not over-mix. Wash the cranberries, removing any stems or wrinkled cranberries. Leave them whole, or chop them and add to the batter.

Fill oiled muffin tins to ⅔ capacity and bake for 20 minutes.

VARIATIONS

Substitute blueberries or raisins for cranberries. Add nuts and/or spices.

QUICK-AND-EASY
BRAN MUFFINS

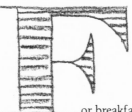or breakfast or brunch, nothing
is more welcome than an honest, sweet, and nutritious bran muffin straight from
the oven. Makes 12 muffins.

1 cup whole wheat pastry flour

1 ¼ cups wheat bran ❖ *1 teaspoon non-aluminum baking powder*

¼ teaspoon sea salt ❖ *1 to 2 tablespoons corn oil*

⅓ cup barley malt syrup ❖ *1 cup water*

Preheat the oven to 335° F. Mix the dry ingredients together. Combine the wet
ingredients and add to the dry ingredients, mixing just until the batter is moist.
Spoon the batter into lightly oiled muffin tins. Bake about 25 minutes.

NOTE: When using dried fruits (including raisins), soak the fruit for 1 hour or
simmer for 10 minutes in water to cover. Use this soaking or cooking water
instead of the water called for in the recipe above.

VARIATIONS

Add any of the following to Basic Bran Muffins:

½ cup raisins ❖ *½ cup chopped dates*

½ cup chopped dried peaches ❖ *½ cup chopped dried apricots*

½ cup chopped pecans ❖ *½ cup chopped walnuts*

7

CREPES

BASIC EGGLESS CREPES

 simple crepe for those avoiding eggs, this basic recipe can be accompanied by any one of many delicious fillings. Makes about 20 crepes.

2 cups whole wheat pastry flour ❖ *¼ teaspoon sea salt*

apple juice to form batter ❖ *oil for pan*

Roast the flour by placing in a dry skillet and stirring constantly over a medium heat until the flour is golden and fragrant.

Combine the flour and salt. Add enough juice to form a thin batter. For best results, set the batter aside for 1 to 8 hours — the longer the better.

Heat a skillet or crepe pan and brush it with oil. Test the heat of the pan by dropping a bit of batter into the skillet — when it sizzles and bubbles, the pan is ready. Use a ladle to spoon just enough batter into the pan to cover the bottom. Lift and tilt the pan, moving the pan around quickly in a circular motion, until the inside bottom of the pan is completely covered with batter. Cook the crepe over a medium heat until tiny holes begin to appear on its surface. Remove by turning the pan upside down and flipping the crepe onto a cloth. Fill immediately with any one of the following:

Fruit Compote ❖ *Applesauce*
Apple Butter ❖ *Puréed Winter Squash*

Place the filling down the center of the crepe, and fold the top and bottom over it.

84

BUCKWHEAT CREPES

 welcome change for breakfast, lunch, or dinner, these hearty buckwheat crepes can also enliven a lunchbox or picnic meal. Makes 8 large crepes.

2 cups buckwheat flour

¼ cup whole wheat pastry flour

¼ teaspoon sea salt

4 cups water

Mix all ingredients into a batter and set aside to rest for 45 minutes. Heat a small skillet or crepe pan. The pan is ready when a drop of water sizzles on it.

NOTE: A well-seasoned skillet requires oiling for the first crepe only. However, if the crepes are sticking to the pan, lightly oil it before pouring the batter for each crepe.

Transfer the batter to a large measuring cup or pitcher. Pour a small amount of batter onto the skillet, then lift the skillet and rotate to spread the batter thinly and evenly. Cook the crepe over a medium heat for 3 to 4 minutes, then turn it over and cook for 2 minutes more.

FILLINGS
Squash Purée ❖ *Fruit Butters* ❖ *Maple Cream*

The addition of oil and eggs makes Valentine Crepes a richer variety of the crepe, suitable as a dessert with Valentine Strawberry Sauce (page 98), or as a main dish with a savory filling. Makes about 25 crepes.

2 cups whole wheat pastry flour

¼ cup plus 1 tablespoon corn oil

½ teaspoon sea salt

2½ cups water

3 eggs

Combine all ingredients in a bowl or blender and whisk or blend thoroughly until smooth.

Heat a 9-inch skillet or crepe pan over medium-high heat and brush with a very small amount of oil. Pour in 3½ to 4 tablespoons of batter, immediately lifting and tilting the pan so that the batter evenly coats the entire bottom.

Cook the crepe for 2 minutes or until the edges are golden and begin to pull away from the sides of the pan. The top should be almost dry and slightly bubbly. Turn the crepe over and cook for 1 to 2 minutes on the other side. Crepes may be may be prepared well ahead of filling and serving time, if stacked with a light cotton towel between them.

To fill, spread 3 tablespoons of filling across the center. Fold over the top and bottom, and garnish with a little more of the filling, if desired.

FILLINGS

Valentine Strawberry Sauce (page 98)

Applesauce

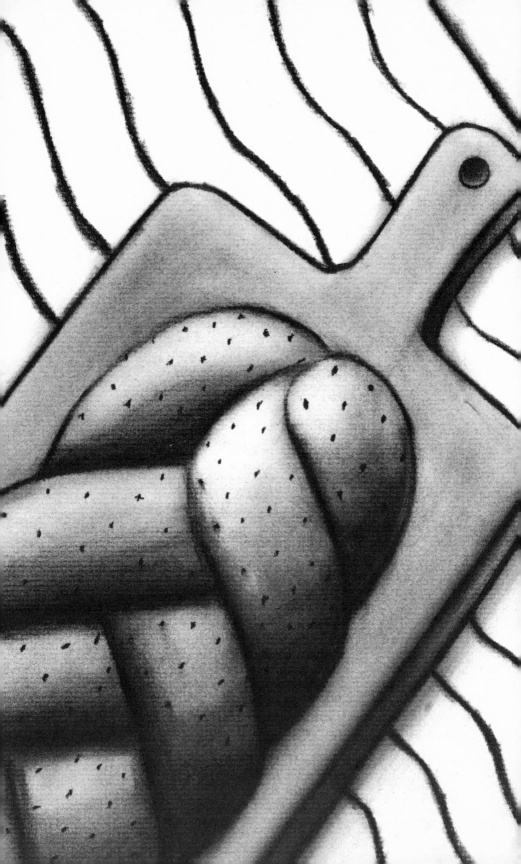

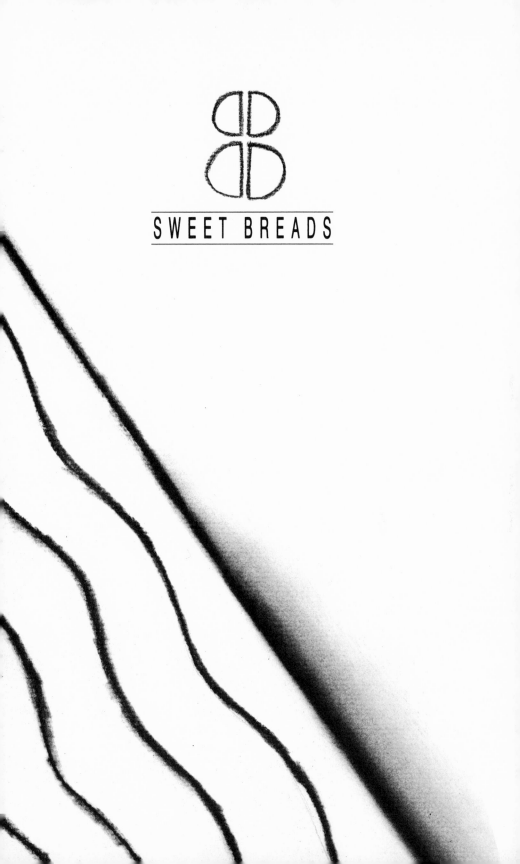

SWEET BREADS

FILLED BRAIDED BREAD

*t*he filling for this bread can be varied ad infinitum. In addition to the raisin/cinnamon mixture below, strawberry jam and crushed toasted almonds are a favorite combination. Makes 2 large, braided loaves.

3 cups warm water

2 tablespoons barley malt syrup ❖ *2 tablespoons corn oil*

1 tablespoon granulated yeast ❖ *3 to 4 cups whole wheat bread flour*

3 cups unbleached white flour ❖ *1½ teaspoons sea salt*

¾ cup white raisins ❖ *¾ cup currants*

1 cup water ❖ *¼ teaspoon cinnamon*

2 tablespoons maple syrup (optional)

NOTE: Cake yeast or nugget yeast must be "proofed" before using. To proof the yeast, place it in a small bowl. Combine 1 cup warm water with the barley malt syrup, and sprinkle it over the yeast. Stir. Let it rest until the yeast dissolves and begins to bubble. The bubbling indicates that the yeast is "active."

Combine the water, barley malt, oil, yeast, and 2 cups whole wheat flour in a large mixing bowl. Whisk for 1 minute to blend all the ingredients. If you are using cake or nugget yeast which has been "proofed," add 2 cups water instead of 3 and use 1 tablespoon barley malt syrup instead of 2.

Mix together 3 cups unbleached white flour, 1 cup whole wheat flour, and the salt. Add to wet ingredients and mix well until the dough has formed a ball in the center of the bowl. If the dough looks wet, mix in the remaining cup of flour as needed.

Turn the dough out onto a lightly floured work surface and begin kneading, using any extra flour to keep the dough from sticking to the work area while you knead. Knead the dough for 4 to 5 minutes, then place it in a lightly oiled bowl. Cover the bowl with a damp towel and set it aside to allow the dough to rise until doubled in size, about 1½ hours in a warm room.

While the dough is rising, heat the raisins, currants, and 1 cup water to boiling, then reduce the heat and simmer for 10 minutes. Set aside. Punch the dough down, then cover again and set it aside to rise for about 30 minutes. Punch the dough down a second time and set it aside to rest for a few minutes.

Preheat the oven to 350° F.

Divide the dough into 6 equal pieces, which will be used in 2 loaves. Set 3 pieces aside. Roll each ball of dough out into a rectangle 16 to 18 inches long and 5 to 6 inches wide. Drain any excess water from the fruit, and spoon $1/6$ of the fruit the length of the dough. Sprinkle lightly with cinnamon. Roll up the rectangle lengthwise to form a long filled roll. Pinch the seam and ends to seal them, and set aside until all 3 pieces of dough have been formed into filled rolls. Place all 3 rolls side by side on the cookie sheet and pinch the tops together to form one piece at the top while keeping the rolls separate. Begin to braid the rolls, keeping some tension in each roll while lifting and turning it, but always pushing each roll up towards the top to make a full-braided loaf.

Repeat the filling and rolling with the remaining 3 pieces of dough to make the second loaf.

Let the loaves rise for about 40 minutes at room temperature, or until no impression remains when your finger is pressed onto the dough.

Bake the breads for 35 minutes, or until they are nicely browned. The loaves should sound hollow when rapped on the bottom.

ANGIE'S
OUTRAGEOUS BANANA BREAD

*g*rain coffee and tofu enhance the creamy sweetness of bananas, in a bread as easy to make as it is luscious. Makes 1 loaf.

1 cup unbleached white flour

1 cup whole wheat pastry flour, sifted

1½ teaspoons non-aluminum baking powder ❖ *½ teaspoon sea salt*

1 teaspoon instant grain coffee granules dissolved in ½ cup water

⅓ cup corn oil ❖ *⅔ cup maple syrup* ❖ *4 oz. soft tofu*

1 teaspoon vanilla extract ❖ *2 ripe bananas*

½ cup walnuts (optional)

Preheat the oven to 375° F.

Sift the dry ingredients into a large bowl. Place the liquid ingredients, including the bananas, into a blender and process until smooth. Add the wet ingredients to the dry ingredients and mix well. Add the nuts.

Oil a bread loaf pan and fill it with the batter. Bake for 45-55 minutes. The banana bread is done when a toothpick inserted into the center comes out dry.

EASY
LEMON-WALNUT BREAD

lmost foolproof, and very tasty. Flavored with walnuts and lemon zest, this quick bread is perfect for tea-time nibbling. Makes 1 loaf or 24 muffins.

½ cup walnuts ❖ *¼ cup lemon juice*

grated peel of two lemons ❖ *½ cup apple juice* ❖ *½ cup corn oil*

½ cup maple syrup ❖ *2 cups whole wheat pastry flour*

2 teaspoons non-aluminum baking powder

pinch sea salt

Preheat the oven to 375° F.

Roast and chop the walnuts and set them aside. Grate and squeeze the lemons. Whip the rind and lemon juice together with the apple juice, oil, and maple syrup. Sift together the flour, baking powder, and salt.

Combine the wet ingredients with the dry, and mix a smooth batter. Fold in the walnuts. Pour the batter into a lightly oiled bread loaf pan, or fill paper-lined muffin tins two-thirds full. Bake for 15 minutes. Reduce the heat to 350° F, and continue to bake for 20 minutes more. Set aside to cool. Remove bread from the pan, and slice gently with a serrated knife. Serve with Apricot Spread (page 99).

SAUCES, FILLINGS & FROSTINGS

CRANBERRY SAUCE

lthough cranberry sauce
is now usually cooked only briefly, simmering for a long time deepens the flavor
and creates a more old-fashioned condiment. Makes 6 cups.

6 cups cranberries

½ teaspoon sea salt

2 cups apple cider or juice

½ cup rice malt syrup

⅔ cup barley malt syrup

peel of one tangerine, grated lightly

In a saucepan, combine all the ingredients except the tangerine peel. Simmer for
1 to 3 hours. Add the tangerine peel for the last half-hour of cooking.

CHERRY SAUCE

*D*ark juicy cherries simmered in apple juice make an exceptionally beautiful topping for rice puddings, cakes, or Tofu Cheesecake (page 41). Makes about 2½ cups.

1 teaspoon kuzu,
dissolved in ¼ cup cold water

2 cups apple juice ❖ *1 cup pitted cherries*

pinch sea salt

rice malt syrup (optional), to taste

Dissolve the kuzu in ¼ cup water and combine with the remaining ingredients in a saucepan. Bring to a simmer over a medium-low heat and stir constantly for 2 to 3 minutes or until the mixture is thick and glossy.

Serve the sauce warm, on cool Rice a l' Amande (page 27) or use it with any favorite recipe that needs a fruit glaze.

VALENTINE
STRAWBERRY SAUCE

Valentine Strawberry Sauce is the perfect match for Valentine Crepes (page 86), and an exciting partner for muffins or cakes. Makes about 3 cups.

2-1 pound bags frozen unsweetened strawberries,
or 1 quart fresh berries

½ cup maple syrup or rice malt syrup

3 tablespoons arrowroot powder, dissolved in
¼ cup cold water

Place the strawberries and syrup in a covered saucepan and heat just to boiling. Immediately reduce heat and uncover the pot. When the strawberries are tender, but still retaining their bright color, stir in the dissolved arrowroot. Stir constantly over a medium heat for a few minutes, or until the sauce is thick and glossy. Remove from the heat immediately. Serve hot or chilled.

APRICOT
SAUCE OR SPREAD

pricot sauce enhances the flavor of Easy Lemon-Walnut Bread (page 93), and is also heavenly when spread on warm toast.

½ pound dried apricots

apple juice — enough to cover apricots, plus 1 cup

1 tablespoon arrowroot powder

pinch sea salt

Simmer the apricots in the apple juice to cover until soft, then purée them in a blender or food mill, or chop very fine.

In a saucepan, dissolve the arrowroot in 1 cup apple juice and bring to a simmer over medium-low heat. Add the puréed apricots and stir constantly until the mixture thickens. Add the salt and remove from the heat.

MISO
"MINCEMEAT"

iso's strong, rich flavor is the essence of this dessert. Miso "mincemeat" can also be spread on toast, served like chutney with curried dishes, or used as a filling for pies or turnovers.

4 tart apples — peeled, cored, and diced

½ cup apple juice

1½ cups raisins

grated rind of 1 orange

2 cups nut meats, preferably walnuts

2 tablespoons hatcho miso, or 1½ tablespoons red or barley miso

¼ teaspoon cinnamon

¼ to ½ teaspoon cloves, allspice, or coriander

Combine the first five ingredients in a heavy pot, bring to a boil, and simmer for 30 minutes. Dilute the miso in a little of the cooking liquid, and stir until creamy. Add the miso and the seasonings to the pot. Mix well and remove from the heat. Allow the mixture to cool to room temperature before using.

SQUASH JAM

A n old-fashioned vegetable
spread that's sure to please the whole family. Naturally sweet winter squash is
enlivened with the flavor of orange and lemon. Makes about 4 cups.

4 cups winter squash or pumpkin — peeled and grated

½ orange (juice and lightly grated rind)

½ lemon (juice and lightly grated rind)

1½ cups maple syrup or honey

½ teaspoon sea salt

Combine all ingredients in a heavy saucepan over medium-low heat. Bring to a
simmer, stirring constantly. Reduce heat to low and stir frequently until the
mixture is thick and smooth. While the jam is still very hot, spoon it into hot,
sterilized jars and seal.

Set aside for one to two weeks before using, to allow the flavors to blend. Store
in a cool place.

CURRANT FROSTING

immered, puréed currants are combined with tahini to yield a creamy spread. Use it as a cake frosting, or as a luscious topping for toast or muffins. Makes about 1½ cups.

2 cups currants

water to cover currants ❖ *1 tablespoon tahini*

poppyseeds, for garnish

Simmer the currants in water to cover for 30 minutes. Drain, and reserve the liquid. Place the currants, tahini, and 2 tablespoons of the currant cooking liquid in a blender or suribachi and blend thoroughly. Let the frosting cool before using. Sprinkle with poppyseeds.

INSTANT
TOFU MOCHA CREME

his all-purpose creme filling can serve as a filling for tarts, strudels, turnovers, or between layers of cake, or as a topping for Carob Brownies (page 67). Makes about 1 cup.

¼ cup raisin purée

1 cup soft-style tofu

3 tablespoons almond butter

1 tablespoon instant grain coffee granules

pinch sea salt

To make raisin purée, simmer ½ cup raisins in water to cover for 20 minutes. Drain the raisins, reserving the cooking liquid for another use. Purée the raisins in a blender until smooth.

Squeeze the water from the tofu. Combine the tofu and the raisin purée in a suribachi or blender and process until creamy. Add the almond butter and grain coffee granules and continue to blend on low speed until the entire mixture is of a uniform consistency.

TOFU
"WHIPPED CREAM"

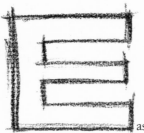asiest to prepare of all the spreads, tofu "whipped cream" is also one of the most versatile. Use it as you would the dairy version. Makes about 1 cup.

8 oz. soft-style tofu

½ cup rice malt syrup ❖ *1 tablespoon safflower oil*

½ teaspoon vanilla extract

pinch sea salt

Combine all ingredients in a blender and process until smooth. This may be flavored by substituting citrus rind for the vanilla, or by folding in your favorite nuts.

10

CANDIES & SNACKS

POPPED CORN DELIGHT

barley malt syrup lends an old-fashioned caramel flavor to this nutritious popcorn and peanuts snack.

10 cups popped corn

sea salt, to taste

¾ cup barley malt syrup, or just enough to make the popcorn stick together

1 to 2 cups roasted peanuts

Lightly salt the corn after popping. Heat the barley malt in a double boiler or heavy saucepan until it begins to foam. Remove it from the heat. Mix the popcorn and peanuts in a large bowl. Pour the hot barley malt over them and mix well using two large spoons. Rub a small amount of oil into your hands and spread the mixture on two lightly oiled baking sheets. Bake at 300° F for 10 minutes.

Popped Corn Delight is done when it is no longer sticky to the touch. Remove from the oven and spread on sheets of waxed paper to dry.

VARIATION

To make popcorn balls, prepare popcorn and barley malt as for Popped Corn Delight. Before baking, form the popcorn and hot barley malt mixture into balls 2 inches in diameter. Bake as directed.

STUFFED DATES

*S*tuffed dates are a welcome addition to holiday buffets. Packed in decorated tins, they make an appreciated gift, and children love to help prepare them.

1 pound large dates

1 cup walnuts, roasted and chopped fine

1 tablespoon miso (red or kome) ❖ *1 tablespoon barley malt syrup*

1 tablespoon tahini ❖ *cinnamon*

1 lemon (grated rind and juice)

Pit the dates. To roast the walnuts, spread them on a cookie sheet and place in a 325° F oven for 10 to 15 minutes. Set aside to cool, then chop.

Combine the miso, barley malt syrup, tahini, cinnamon, and lemon juice and rind. Blend well and stir in the chopped walnuts. Stuff the pitted dates with this mixture.

HALVAH

An easy-to-prepare sweet that is a nutritious, high-energy food as well. Halvah is an excellent hiking and camping staple.

¼ cup tahini

¼ cup rice malt syrup

1 teaspoon grated orange or lemon rind

pinch sea salt ❖ ⅓ cup matzah meal

*¼ cup toasted sesame seeds, slightly crushed, or
toasted unsweetened coconut*

Roast the tahini in a small skillet over a low heat for two minutes, stirring constantly. Remove from the heat when the tahini changes color and develops a stronger aroma.

Use a spatula to quickly scoop the tahini into a small mixing bowl. (If the tahini remains in the hot skillet it will overcook and may burn.) Add the rice malt syrup, citrus rind, and salt. Mix well and stir in the matzah meal. Roll by teaspoons into balls, and roll each ball in sesame seeds or coconut. Store in a covered container.

VARIATION

Halvah, with the matzah meal omitted from the recipe, may also be used as a spread for crackers or rice cakes.

MARZIPAN

arzipan is a traditional European candy, and now you can make it yourself, with rice malt syrup as sweetener. Use it also as a filling for breads (see Filled Braided Bread, page 90) or other pastries. Makes approximately one-half pound.

1 cup whole almonds

3 tablespoons rice malt syrup

1 to 2 drops bitter almond extract

Boil the almonds in water to cover for 2 to 3 minutes. Drain, then rinse briefly in cold water to cool, and rub between the palms of your hand to remove the skins. Mix the blanched almonds with the rice malt syrup and bitter almond extract. Blend a small amount at a time in a blender or food processor until the paste is smooth enough to form into small shapes.

For a fancy touch, dust with carob powder or color with beet juice.

CRUNCH,
COOKIES, OR GRANOLA MIX

The basic recipe for crunch topping that can be baked over fruit, made into cookies, or eaten as a breakfast cereal. The recipe can be increased simply by doubling the ingredients. Makes 4 cups Crunch.

3 cups rolled oats

1½ cups whole wheat pastry flour or oat flour

½ teaspoon sea salt ❖ ½ cup corn oil

½ cup maple syrup or rice malt syrup

1 teaspoon vanilla extract

ADDITIONS FOR COOKIES

1 cup roasted chopped walnuts ❖ ⅓ cup water

*1 teaspoon grated lemon or orange rind or
pinch of ground fennel*

ADDITIONS FOR GRANOLA

1 to 1½ cups combined dried fruits, nuts, and seeds, such as:

currants ❖ chopped dried pears ❖ walnut halves

pecan halves ❖ sunflower seeds

sesame seeds ❖ pinch of cinnamon

NOTE: If sesame seeds are used, they should be washed, drained, and dry-roasted before adding to the other ingredients.

Preheat the oven to 350° F. For crumb topping, combine the dry ingredients, mix in the oil with a wooden spoon, then add the syrup and vanilla. The mixture should have the texture of a dry dough and break easily into small clumps. Spread on a cookie sheet and bake the crunch approximately 12 minutes, or until evenly browned. During this time, turn the mixture twice with a spatula.

To make baked fruit with topping, crumble the topping over sliced raw apples or other fresh fruit. Cover with foil, bake 30 minutes, then remove the foil. Continue to bake for an additional 8 to 10 minutes to let the topping become crisp.

To make cookies, follow the recipe above, adding 1 cup roasted chopped walnuts to the dry ingredients. Add the water and flavoring after mixing in the maple syrup. (Omit the vanilla in the original recipe if another flavoring is used.) Drop by spoonfuls onto a lightly oiled cookie sheet, and shape into rounds approximately ¼-inch thick. Bake for 18 to 20 minutes at 350° F. Remove to cool on a wire rack and store in a tightly covered container. Use your choice of fruits and nuts, and flavorings other than vanilla, to vary the taste.

To make granola, follow the original recipe and vary additional ingredients. Chop the nuts or leave them whole. Sunflower seeds and sesame seeds should be dry-roasted before combining with other ingredients.

YAM DROPS

oasted chestnut flour is the sweet topping for an unusual autumn dessert: deep-fried golden balls of orange-seasoned yams.

4 cups cooked yams (about 8 medium yams)

2 tablespoons tahini

2 tablespoons maple syrup

1 teaspoon vanilla extract

1 teaspoon lightly grated orange rind

½ teaspoon sea salt

finely crumbled bread crumbs, cake crumbs, or cookie crumbs

1 egg, beaten ❖ oil for deep-frying

chestnut flour

Bake the whole yams at 375° F for 45 to 60 minutes. Remove the skins and mash the yam meat. Place the mashed yams in a saucepan and cook over a low heat, stirring often until the yams are very dry. Add the tahini, maple syrup, vanilla, orange rind, and salt.

Shape into balls, 1 inch in diameter, and chill them for at least 1 hour or until they are firm. Roll the balls in the crumbs, dip into the beaten egg, and roll in crumbs again. Deep-fry until golden. Sprinkle with toasted chestnut flour and serve immediately.

NOTE: To toast the chestnut flour, place it in a small, dry skillet over medium-low heat and stir constantly until it is fragrant.

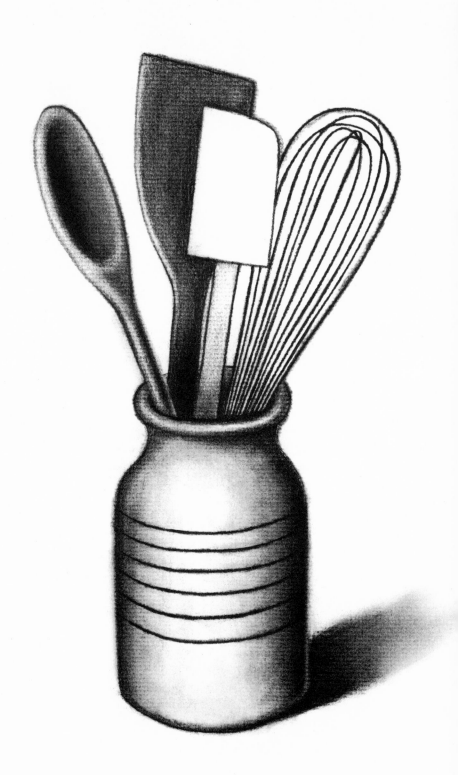

GLOSSARY

AGAR   Flakes or bars derived from a sea vegetable used as a gelling agent; also called kanten.

AMAZAKE   A sweet pudding or beverage of cooked grains that have been fermented for a short time with koji (grain that has been inoculated with *Aspergillus oryzae* mold).

ARROWROOT STARCH   Arrowroot is a tropical perennial with swollen starchy rhizomes (underground stems). The starch, in very fine grains which are easily digestible, is particularly suitable for children or sick people. It is used as a thickening agent, similar to cornstarch or kuzu.

BARLEY MALT SYRUP   A thick, dark brown sweetener made from sprouted barley or a combination of barley and corn.

BASMATI RICE   An aromatic variety of long grain brown or white rice.

BROWN RICE   Whole, unpolished rice, the form white rice is in before it is separated from its bran and germ. Brown rice is available in many varieties, including short, medium, and long grain, sweet rice, rice flakes, and aromatic rice.

CAROB   The pod of tamarind or St. John's Bread, used as an alternative to chocolate. Carob is most often found in the form of roasted or unroasted powder.

CHESTNUT FLOUR   A very fine powder made from ground dried chestnuts. It has a sweet taste and is a pleasant addition to cookies and other desserts. Chestnut flour may be found in Oriental and Middle Eastern markets, and in some natural foods stores.

COUSCOUS A staple dish of northern Africa consisting of a grain topped with vegetables and a spicy sauce. In the U.S., a refined semolina is commonly marketed as couscous.

CORN FLOUR Ground from dried corn kernels, corn flour has a much finer texture than cornmeal.

KANTEN See Agar.

KOJI See Amazake.

KUZU A white starch made from the root of the Japanese kuzu plant, called "kudzu" in this country.

MAPLE GRANULES Produced from Dark Amber or Grade B maple syrup by a vacuum drying process. The resulting sugar is milled and screened to separate fine powder from the granules. The powder is sold to commercial processors and the granules are reserved for home use.

MAPLE SYRUP The concentrated sap of maple trees.

MISO A fermented grain or bean paste made from ingredients such as soybeans, barley, and rice. Many varieties are now available.

MOCHIKO (SWEET RICE FLOUR) A high gluten flour made from very finely ground sweet rice. It can be used like rice flour although sweet rice flour has a softer and stickier texture.   Japanese sweet rice flour is less glutinous than the Chinese variety.

OLIVE OIL Olive oil is unique in that it is the only oil readily available that can be considered cold-pressed. The best oil comes from olives that are hand-picked just before they are fully ripe. The first extraction is a simple, gentle pressing that doesn't heat the oil much above room temperature. Oil obtained from this first pressing receives no further treatment other than filtering to remove pulp. This oil is labeled "virgin olive oil" and is the only oil that can be labeled as such. Lesser-quality olive oils are designated only as "pure."

Virgin olive oil comes in three grades. "Extra virgin" has perfect flavor and aroma, "fine virgin" has the same flavor as "extra" but a high acidity, and "plain virgin" oil, the grade most often sold in the U.S., is imperfect in flavor and has the highest acidity.

Pure olive oil has excellent stability and can sometimes be stored without refrigeration for over a year, but virgin oils degrade more quickly. Most of the unsaturates in olive oil are in the form of monounsaturated oleic acid, instead of the lighter polyunsaturate linoleic, which amounts to only 15 percent. This results in a heavier and more fatty oil.

POLENTA / CORNMEAL Cornmeal (known as *polenta* in Italy) is usually milled from yellow dent corn, but occasionally from flint or flour corn. Cornmeal is used for corn bread and cornmeal mush. It can be combined with wheat flour in bread recipes to produce a slightly crumbly, crunchy sweet loaf.

RICE MALT SYRUP A sweet, thick syrup made from brown rice and barley.

ROASTED OR TOASTED NUTS Spread whole nuts on a baking sheet and place in a preheated 350° F. oven for 10 to 15 minutes or until fragrant. Stir occasionally. Always roast nuts before chopping them.

SAFFLOWER OIL Safflower oil has the highest percentage of unsaturated fats of all the oils (94 percent) and is highest in linoleic acid (78 percent). Since unsaturated fats become rancid more quickly than saturated fats, one drawback of high unsaturation is short shelf life. Safflower oil may be refrigerated to retard rancidity. It can be used for deep-frying.

SEA SALT Salt extracted from sea water and minimally refined. It contains no additives and has very small amounts of trace elements, making it moderately superior to other types of salt.

SEMOLINA A granular, milled durum wheat flour used chiefly in the production of pasta.

SOYMILK Beverages made from soybeans with a flavor and consistency similar to dairy milk.

SURIBACHI A serrated, glazed clay bowl. Used with a pestle, called a *surikogi*, for grinding and puréing foods.

TAHINI A smooth paste made from ground white sesame seeds.

TOASTED OR DARK SESAME OIL Made in Japan from whole sesame seeds that have first been carefully toasted then pressed to extract their flavorful oil. No chemicals are used in the processing and, since this oil contains the natural preservatives vitamin E, lecithin, and sesamol, no artificial preservatives are added. Like other natural unrefined oils, toasted sesame oil should be stored in a cool, dark place.

TOASTED SESAME SEEDS Prepared by heating sesame seeds in a frying pan, over a medium heat, and stirring constantly until they begin to pop and are very fragrant. Do not allow them to burn. The are completely toasted when you can reduce them to a powder by rubbing a few gently between thumb and third finger.

TOFU Soybean curd, made from soybeans and a coagulant.

WHEAT Wheat is available in hard and soft varieties. The hard wheats contain higher levels of protein than the soft wheats, and the soft wheats contain higher levels of carbohydrates. Both hard and soft wheats are further classified into spring or winter varieties, referring to the season in which they are planted, and by color — usually red or white.

The hard wheats, because of their higher gluten (protein) content, are the basic bread wheats. Generally the hard spring wheats tend to have a bit more gluten than the hard winter wheats.

Soft wheat varieties do not rise as well as the hard wheats, and are used in making pastries or blended with the harder varieties for bread baking. Pastry wheat, a white spring variety that is very low in gluten content, is used for crackers or pastry dough. Some pastry wheat is exported to Japan for making noodles.